The Franchise Investment Guide

How to find a high-quality franchise that can give you everything you want in life

Dru Carpenito

Copyright © 2019 by Dru Carpenito

All rights reserved. Reproduction of this work beyond that permitted by Section 107 or 108 or the 1976 United State Copyright Act without express written permission of the copyright owner is unlawful. Requests for permission or further information should be addressed to Dru Carpenito (www.DruCarpenito.com)

This publication is designed to provide accurate and authoritative information in regard to the subject matter covered. It is sold with the understand that the publisher is not engaged in rendering legal, accounting, or other professional services. If legal advice or other expert assistance is required, the services of a competent professional person should be sought.

IMPORTANT!
READ THIS FIRST!

Dear Friend,

Your decision to get this guide is probably going to turn out to be one of the smartest moves you've made.

As you are about to learn, this guide totally delivers and will arm you with a plan and knowledge that you can use to cut through all of the clutter and noise on the internet to find high-quality franchises and then dissect them to figure out which one is the best fit for you. What I'm about to share with you is a proven process that **hundreds** of **successful** franchise owners have used over the years to invest in, build, grow, and then sell (as in cash out) successful franchise businesses.

Consider this: The simple secrets in this guide have helped hundreds of people invest in the right franchise that offered them the lifestyle and financial opportunity that they literally only dreamt about.

For example: I helped a husband and wife team build an education franchise that allowed them to work **less than ten hours per week** with a cash flow equivalent to that of a 50+ hour per week senior-executive level position. SIDE NOTE: They then sold this business (with a little help from yours truly) for a significant premium.

Another example: A successful entrepreneur wanted to expand his portfolio of small businesses and create an additional income stream. By following the same process I outline in this guide and working together with me, he found just what he was looking for and invested in a manager-run hair care franchise. He now owns **fifteen** locations of this brand and he's _not_ cutting anyone's hair.

Another example: A corporate executive who wanted to diversify his household income and build an exit plan from corporate America followed my process and guidance and invested in a manager-run franchise in the boutique fitness industry. He is opening three locations over the next couple of years **while he keeps his job** and will have a cash-generating asset to walk into when he's ready to leave his W-2 gig.

Another example: An engineer was laid off and refused to go back into the corporate world, so he reached out to me for guidance. He found a restoration business that he had zero industry experience with yet built a successful business that he sold (and cashed out) and **retired.**

You see, I help people who are serious about changing their lives and opening their own business. The quick story on me is that I've helped a few hundred people invest in, build, grow and sell (as in cash out) franchises in my career. I've spent my entire career in franchising and everything you are about to read is based on real-world, from-the-trenches experience from everyone I've ever worked with in franchising.

Today, I help my private candidates through a no-cost service explore if there is a franchise out there that is a fit to help them achieve their financial and lifestyle goals. I help them find a high-quality franchise that gives them the absolute highest, and I mean highest, opportunity to achieve everything they want from their own successful business. The reason people want my help is because finding a high-quality franchise that fits what they want is a lot harder than it sounds. The folks who reach out to me for help want me to help guide them in the right direction (not to mention save them **a lot** of time cutting through the noise on the internet).

You've probably experienced the noise I'm talking about. If you haven't already, go to Entrepreneur.com or any of the other multitude of franchise directories and you'll see the franchises on there all claiming the same thing:

"A proven business model in a multi-trillion, no gazillion, dollar industry!"

"Get in at the ground floor of this franchise!"

"Ranked X in [insert name of ranking]"
(which no one outside of the franchise world knows about)

Blah, blah, blah…

Do you know what I'm talking about?

How in the world is someone supposed to understand what any of the information on the internet about franchises actually means? Or figure out which high-quality franchises to dive in and research is mind boggling to me.

Not to jump ahead, but one of the most important steps to take in finding and researching high-quality franchises you'll learn about is to compare them to one another (just like you do when you buy a house). And, just like going out to see houses you think may be a fit, getting good solid information about franchises to then compare to one another takes time (and the information you need isn't what is being advertised on the internet). You need to be picky. But first, you need to understand what you want so when you find it…BINGO!

Franchising and business ownership can be absolutely amazing. In fact, I believe entrepreneurship is one of the most powerful and significant financial and personal opportunities available to us.

The lifestyle and financial upsides are endless - you control your own comp plan, you work on your own terms, and you set the boundaries.

You call the shots - there are no meetings about meetings, you don't have to deal with headwinds that follow a merger or acquisition, and you're not going to lay yourself off.

There is also a **huge benefit** to building a successful business that most people don't think about and that's the fact that when you have a successful business, you have a cash flowing asset that someone will pay you a **healthy premium** for (it's like a 401(k) plan...only *better*).

Investing in a franchise can be even more amazing!
(when it's done the _right_ way)

The bottom line is investing in a high-quality franchise has all of the upsides and it can lower your risk significantly.

And I'm **not** talking about fast food franchises. What I am talking about are high-quality franchises that savvy and motivated people with no direct industry experience can succeed with. And when I say "high-quality," I'm talking about franchises that:

- Have a unique business that has proven to be successful and profitable.
- Have engineered a lot of horsepower "under the hood" around tools, technology and support that would be very hard (and expensive) to build on your own.

What all of this means to you is this: investing in a high-quality franchise can help you build your own successful business faster (and cheaper) than doing it on your own.

However (and this is a **big** "however"), business ownership and franchise ownership **isn't** for everyone. Investing in the right franchise will undoubtedly help you build your business faster and maximize your odds of achieving your lifestyle and financial goals. But, simply investing in a franchise is **not** a magic bullet to reap the benefits of success. Whatever franchise you decide to invest in will take hard work, money, and sacrifice. Now, if you do it the right way, the hard work, money, and sacrifice will all be short-term (and **worth it**)! And, in the long run, you will build the business to a point where you can actually enjoy the rewards you set out to achieve.

Now, back to my point in why I'm sharing all of this valuable insight with you for free...

But First, I have a little confession: I may have contributed to a little bit (just a wee bit) of that noise on the internet. For over a decade, I successfully franchised two businesses - one here in the States and one internationally (both of which are pretty high up on the rankings that don't really mean that much). During that time, I helped a few hundred people invest in, build, grow and sell (as in cash out), franchises with the two brands that I was an executive with. A few years ago, my wife and I started a young family and were blessed with twins (a boy and a girl…and, no, they're not identical…you'd be surprised how many times we get that question). Anyway, traveling the world wasn't the most lifestyle-friendly gig with a young family. So I started to think about a career change.

My "AHA" Moment

I remember my "aha" moment clear as day. I was on a business trip in Toronto and I got a call from my wife. I couldn't take the call because I was knee deep in a meeting. A few minutes later, I got a text from her: "call me ASAP." I knew something was up because she doesn't send a text like that unless it's serious. I still remember the feeling I had running through my body as I was wondering what could be wrong.

When I finally was able to call her, she delivered the news. And it hit me like a punch in the gut. I felt powerless and guilty. All I wanted was to be home with my family and I couldn't because I was in a different country. When I got on the first plane home…that's when my mindset about my career changed forever. I realized my family and I had crafted our lifestyle around my job and it didn't have to be that way. I knew there was a better way. A way where travel wouldn't keep me away from my family. A way where I could still provide a comfortable living for them and be present.

So, I started the exact same process that I'm about to share with you.

During my research, I realized the answer was staring me right in the face. I had personally seen the lifestyle and financial benefits of the successful franchise owners I was helping. So, after a lot (and I mean a lot), of research and candid conversations with my wife, I finally annoyed her enough to the point where she told me to **do it** or **shut up** (I have an amazing wife)!

So, I did it.

Fast forward to today

Here I am. I chose to become a consultant who helps people figure out if there is a franchise out there for them. I've also taken my own advice and own a franchise here in Charlotte, NC (I like having multiple income streams). I travel twice a year and that's only to meet with founders, CEOs, and executives from high-quality franchises and to attend the annual conference of the franchise we own.

Through my private consulting I help people who are motivated to make a change in their life, by opening their own business, find a franchise that will give them what they want out of life. I work with people from all different walks of the world – from current corporate executives to husband and wife teams, to corporate refugees, to entrepreneurs. The things the folks I work with have in common are what they are seeking to take out of their business and that is **money**, **equity**, **freedom**, and **flexibility**. What they do with their time and money is up to them but they are all serious about putting in the hard work to build a business that enables exactly what they want.

So, I wrote this Franchise Investment Guide and decided to share it with folks who are curious or serious about investing in a franchise. What you are about to read in this guide is a culmination of my first-hand, real-world experience of working belly-to-belly with hundreds of successful franchise owners and entrepreneurs around the world. I've been fortunate to have helped a lot of people enjoy more success and happiness by helping them invest in a franchise that was the right fit.

By following the methodology I share with you, you will become a wiser investor and savvier entrepreneur. You will be armed with the tools to figure out how to determine if there is a franchise out there that can help you get to wherever it is you want to get to in life. Now the methodology is only part of it. The other major piece to your strategy is to make sure you approach this whole thing with the right **mindset**.

Onward to the good stuff.

Thank you for reading my guide,

Sincerely,

P.S. You may be wondering how much I charge for my services or where my pitch is coming in. Well, if you are, please know that my services are **free** to anyone I work with. I'm paid like an executive recruiter to help motivated people find high-quality franchises. If you are serious and motivated and want my help, I will never ask you for a dime and I will never ask you to sign a contract with me. At the end of this guide, I'll share some more information about how you can work with me.

It's a pretty simple pitch:

If you want to figure out if there is a franchise out there for you and you like what I have to say in this guide, then you'll probably like working with me. Plus, it's free. The first step is also pretty simple: we have a conversation and then take it from there.

Onward!

TABLE OF CONTENTS

PART 1: MINDSET

The Entrepreneurial Mindset (13)

What makes entrepreneurs successful? (14)

The Consumer Mindset (15)

Fear and anxiety are a good thing (16)

Other people (16)

Irrational manifestations of fear (17)

PART 2: MONEY!

Cash flow = the lifeblood of a business (20)

Something more important than money (21)

How to figure out how much money you can make (22)

What's your exit strategy? (23)

The three key pieces to funding (26)

Where to get the funding (27)

Using pre-tax retirement money without paying penalties or taxes (27)

Small business loans (28)

Home equity loans (29)

Leasing (29)

Portfolio Loans (29)

PART 3: A LOOK IN THE MIRROR

From banking executive to happy franchise owner (31)

The "AHA" moment (32)

Crossing the mindset chasm (33)

Your WHY (35)

PART 4: BUYING THE RIGHT FRANCHISE

Finding great franchises (38)

More than just fast food (38)

What a great franchise looks like (39)

Before you start, do this (39)

The most important criteria (40)

Where to find great franchises (41)

How to get all the answers to your questions (42)

PART 5: HOW TO BECOME A PRIVATE CANDIDATE

See for yourself (45)

Step #1:

Get In The Right Mindset

> **"Go to school, get good grades, go to college, get a job, work 40 years, sock away 10% for savings each year and retire."**

Sound familiar? It's the conventional career advice that has been ingrained in all of us since we were young.

Ever heard this advice?

"Starting a business is a huge risk. What if it fails? Your money is safer in the stock market. Working for someone else is more secure. Things will change at work eventually, just hang in there."

What about this?

"A successful business is an incoming producing asset that you can sell. In fact, the better the cash flow and the less dependent the business is on you, the more valuable it will be (i.e. the more money a buyer may give you)!"

You see, rarely are we taught about entrepreneurship and what it's really like. Why is that?

I mean, everyone thinks of owning their own business at some point in their life. But only a few actually do it.

What do entrepreneurs do that other people don't?

The answer is: **nothing**.

What they do have is a different **mindset**.

See, entrepreneurs break the mold of the traditional career path. They are not willing to accept that their fate has to be tied to an employer in order to be successful and happy. They revel in the idea that their reality is negotiable and the only way they can negotiate to make it what they want is to have the control to do so. Entrepreneurship tends to be the only option that enables this control. Entrepreneurs understand that there will never be an ideal time to start a business and so they just make it happen.

And what's even more interesting, many entrepreneurs consider owning their own business a heck of a lot **more secure** and **less risky** than working for someone else.

**Successful entrepreneurs know how to
minimize their risk and maximize their upside.**

Now, I get it. Successful entrepreneurs don't just magically become successful because they have this idea that their reality is negotiable. Entrepreneurs take a calculated risk to build a business. They believe in themselves first and foremost, but also spend a lot of time doing research and fact-finding before they start a business. It's not an overnight decision and it's surely not a decision to be taken lightly.

It starts with an idea and is validated through research. In fact, numerous studies have found that entrepreneurs are not the enigmatic risk takers who defy the odds and risk everything on one big idea, product or service and either soar with success or crash and burn. These studies even suggest that entrepreneurs are more risk-averse than most people.

Successful entrepreneurs know how to assess and manage their risk in a potential business venture and, most importantly, they know how to reduce their risk to the greatest extent they possibly can. They do this by relying on the resources available to them through research, education and understanding the skills and energy needed in order for a particular venture to be successful. Then they weigh the information they have and make a decision.

In this guide, I will explain and outline a process that you can use to maximize your potential for success in franchising by finding and selecting a high-quality franchise that is ideal for you and your goals.

Just as successful entrepreneurs do, using the information in this guide will help you minimize your risk and maximize your upside.

Franchising offers a pathway for many people who have the motivation to own their own business and have specific lifestyle, personal and financial goals that only business ownership can help them achieve. People who turn to franchising don't want to have to reinvent the wheel and take the risk of proving a business concept is viable. Investing in a franchise can offer reduced risk along with the proven systems needed to run every aspect of their business.

Onward.

Avoid the consumer mindset…it's a trap!

It's very easy to fall into this trap since the consumer viewpoint is typically all you have initially to judge a business by (besides all of those magnificent claims you see on the internet).

Avoid it. You want to be in the entrepreneurial mindset and look at the business through the lens of the owner. The goal of the research process I share is to systematically understand the core components of a franchise business (i.e. **role of the owner, customer acquisition strategy, financial margins, drivers of success, etc.**) so you have fundamental and objective information to analyze and determine if the business offers you what you want (from the owner's perspective, not the consumer's).

The consumer mindset clouds your lens of objectively evaluating these key ownership components. Recognizing this tendency and managing it is crucial to properly evaluating a franchise.

Think about this: Almost all of the happiest and most successful franchisees I've worked with over the years decided to open a franchise that…

1. They had never heard of…

2. Was a business they had never thought of…

3. And finally, they would have never even researched the business if they just focused on the widget or service the business provided (and basically just judged it by the surface through their consumer mindset).

By following the process I lay out for you, these happy and successful franchisees were able to find a franchise that was an ideal fit. Many of these individuals have gone on to build a life for themselves and their families that they had only dreamt about.

Be ready for fear and anxiety.

If you don't feel anxious or scared about the idea of opening your own business and investing in a franchise, something is wrong. A range of emotions – from excitement to anxiety to fear - will be a big part of this process for you, and that's ok.

The key is being able to manage your emotions appropriately so they don't ruin the process or cloud decision making. In fact, when managed properly, fear and anxiety can become a great motivator.

> "One of the greatest discoveries a man makes, one of his great surprises, is to find he can do what he was afraid he couldn't do." —Henry Ford

Feelings of fear and anxiety are going to be natural in this process. This process will arm you with knowledge that drives clarity around the unknown answers that are creating much of the anxious feelings you will have.

The **best** source of information, that gives you the real-world clarity you want to have about whether or not you can see yourself being successful with a particular franchise, will be speaking to actual franchise owners. They've all been in your shoes and have taken the leap to invest and build a franchise. Approaching them in the right way and getting their insights to your questions is one of the, if not the, most important steps in figuring out if a franchise is right for you. We'll touch on how to go about this productively later in the guide.

Beware of other people.

You're not the only one who is going to have a rush of emotions flowing through them throughout this process. Your spouse is going to be nervous, your family is going to be anxious and your friends are going to be jealous.

You should include your spouse in every step of the process. You want to do this with your spouse, not **to** your spouse.

Your family is NOT doing the research you are doing and will likely have opinions, many of which will be affected by the limiting beliefs or consumer mindset views that you may have had before you started to actually look under the hood and get the facts about franchise businesses.

Your friends are going to be envious of you because you're pursuing something they have only dreamed of and they will probably have a fixed mindset on your decision (unless they've done the same research you have).

Excuses = a manifestation of fear.

Fear and anxiety will manifest itself in different ways. The most common way it appears will be in the form of irrational excuses. I say irrational, because if you follow the process I outline, you will have the answers to these excuses before they manifest. So, if you have the answers and information, yet start to believe the excuses, that's fear and anxiety taking a hold of you.

I've put together some of the top excuses I've seen that were nothing more than fear and anxiety creeping in the process and disrupting the hours of research invested and holding people back from pursuing their dreams. Some of these are also talked about in a book that is worth reading called *The Toilet Paper Entrepreneur* by Mike Michalowicz. And no, the book is not about a toilet paper business. Mike (a fellow alum of Virginia Tech…Go Hokies!) shares some personal insights from his journey of successes and failures in the multiple companies he's built and sold. He's a very successful entrepreneur with a witty tone and crisp advice. It's a good read.

Anyway, onward to the irrational excuses…

1. **"The economy is not strong enough to start a business"** – [My response]…what are the drivers of demand for the product or service the franchise offers? Has the franchisor provided you with demographics in the areas you are looking that you can analyze? Have you talked to franchisees in other markets with similar characteristics to see how their business is performing?

2. **"Entrepreneurship is too risky"** – That's what we're groomed to think from a young age. Arm yourself with knowledge and a growth mindset to eliminate this excuse rationally.

3. **"A job with a big company is far more secure"** - Tell that to the innocent employees of Enron, Arthur Anderson, Bear Stearns and other corporations who laid off thousands of people as a result of the decisions of a few people.

4. **"I'm too old to start a company"** – "Twenty years from now, you will be more disappointed by the things that you didn't do than by the ones you did do. So, throw off the bowlines. Sail away from the safe harbor. Catch the trade winds in your sails. Explore. Dream. Discover." Mark Twain wrote that.

5. **"I'm too young to start a company"** – There is no legal age limit for starting your own company.

6. **"I won't make enough money"** – How do the key drivers of success in a business align with your strengths? Have you been able to talk to franchise owners who you identify with that have been able to build businesses with similar financial goals that you have?

7. **"I don't have the proper education"** – Entrepreneurial success is tied to your mindset, beliefs, actions and hard work – not your scholastics pedigree.

8. **"The competition is too strong"** – What is the track record of the franchise in Item 20 of the FDD (More to come on FDDs later)? What do the franchisees have to say about the market and how they are able to compete with other companies offering similar services?

9. **"I am not ready"** – I agree, you're not. You're never fully ready. This is just a semblance of the other excuses. The only way to figure this out is to jump and do the research and make the decision based on objective information.

10. **"My spouse doesn't want me to"** – Did you work with him/her to craft your WHY? Did you involve him/her in your research and conversations with the franchisor and franchisees? Did he/she go with you to meet the franchisor face-to-face?

Step #2:

Money!

How To Fund Your Franchise and Figure Out How Much You Can Turn That Money Into!

Let's talk about money!

And lets specifically talk about how you multiply the money you invest in a franchise into an income and asset.

From a purely financial perspective, a successful franchise does one thing. And that one thing is to produce **cash flow**.

As you probably know, the cash flow a business produces is determined from what's left over after the operational expenses are deducted from the money that business brought in and before the accountants do their fancy stuff and account for depreciation, amortization, interest, and taxes. You may also hear what I just referred to as "cash flow" as *EBITDA* (Earnings Before Interest, Taxes, Depreciation and Amortization), *owner's benefit*, and some other names. At the end of the day, a business' cash flow is one, if not the, most important indicators of a business' success.

I like to refer to the cash flow as **discretionary cash flow** because what happens with that money is 100% up to the discretion of the owner. You can use it to obviously pay yourself and then with what's left over, you can invest it for retirement (business owners have access to more retirement strategies than W-2 employees do), real estate (you'll see a lot of a business owners also own the building they operate out of), invest in growing their franchise (maybe opening more locations or buying additional territory to expand into), and whatever you want. It's your pre-tax money and you can do with it what you want.

Now, when I talk about cash flow, I'm not talking about "net profit." Again, as you probably know, the number at the bottom of a profit and loss statement your accountant will give you after they work their magic at the end of the year is your "net profit". The reason is business owners pay taxes on their "net profit" (among other things). So, because taxes are paid on "net profits" entrepreneurs want to minimize their "net profit" to the greatest **legal** extent possible.

I repeat, entrepreneurs want to minimize their "net profit" to the greatest legal extent possible.

Side Note: A good small business accountant is worth his or her weight in gold. The best way to find one is to talk to other entrepreneurs you know and then interview all the referrals.

Another Side Note: (actually, it's a disclaimer): I am *not* an accountant. In no way shape or form should you *ever* take any accounting advice from me (besides go find a good accountant). I also recommend you go out and get a good financial advisor who can help you take advantage of the wonderful retirement strategies entrepreneurs have access to.

Now, you're probably asking yourself why I'm spending time differentiating between cash flow and "net profit." Well, it all ties into how you determine what the financial potential of a particular franchise is. Now that I've done my very crude introduction to entrepreneurial math, let's talk about how you figure out what the cash flow potential (not "net profit" potential) is going to be.

You may be thinking that you'll just ask the franchisor directly, right? Seems like a simple and obvious answer and it surely is. The problem is that the franchisors are strictly forbidden from providing you with any expectation whatsoever about how much money you can make by opening one franchise or even multiple. And the great franchises don't cross that line. In fact, they stray very far away from it.

Isn't that funny how a great franchise with some of the most profitable business models can't talk about their outstanding business model's profitability?

It's the reality and it's for everyone's protection. But there is a way to figure it all out. And there is a system to figure it out that I'm about to share with you.

Before that, I want to mention something that is even more important than figuring out how much money a business can make.

And this ties back to your potential happiness as the potential owner of a potentially great franchise. What I'm about to share is the single most important thing to figure out your potential profitability and potential satisfaction as an owner (the great franchises are made up a network of profitable and happy franchise owners).

And that is figuring out **what** actually **drives** the **profitably** of the business. And by "what," I'm talking about the specific **levers** that the franchise owners **pull** to make their business **grow** and produce **cash flow**.

It's different for every franchise. For some it's about finding a great manager, empowering them to be a great leader and cultivating a culture that lets their employees thrive. For other franchises, it's about acquiring and then retaining a customer. For others, it's about providing consistent customer service (which in many cases may be the exception to the norm in their industry). Whatever the case, understand the levers so you can figure out if you'll be happy actually pulling those levers.

Good news though, the franchisor can help you learn about these drivers and levers. And the great franchises will spend a lot of time helping you learn all about the drivers of their business. In fact, the great franchises will help you understand what tools and support they offer to help their franchise owners yank the bejesus out of those levers to make their business go. More on that later.

Back to the financial stuff...

So, how do you figure out the financial potential for a business without being given the information from the franchisor? Two things:

1. Item 19 of the Franchise Disclosure Document (FDD), and
2. Talking to franchise owners of that particular brand

Item 19 of the FDD – Since I haven't mentioned the Franchise Disclosure Document (aka FDD) yet, here is your quick introduction to the FDD. The FDD is a document that all franchisors in the U.S. are required by the Federal Trade Commission to provide to prospective franchise owners. There are 23 items in total that cover a wide range of information. One of the most viewed Items is Item 19 (also knowns as Financial Performance Representations). This is the section where a franchise can publish financial performance information about their franchised and/or corporate locations. It's completely optional.

Well, as you can imagine, the great franchises are happy and proud to publish information about their business model's financial performance. Thus, this is where you look to get some information for yourself around the unit economics of a particular franchise. If a franchise publishes an Item 19, then the rep you are talking to can talk to you about what is disclosed. But a rep or anyone who is a direct representative can't talk to you about what isn't disclosed in the FDD. So, if a franchisor wants the ability to talk unit economics, numbers and money with their candidates, they need to publish what they want to talk about in Item 19 of their FDD. The Item 19 is a source of data, but it's not the most important source. The most important source of making money with a particular franchise is the next thing.

Talking to franchise owners – Here we are at the **holy grail of information** in franchising…the franchise owners themselves. This is where it all comes together for you. This is where the rubber hits the road. This is where you validate everything you've learned (and in franchising you'll hear speaking to franchise owners referred to as the "validation step" because it's just that – a chance to confirm everything you've learned about the franchise and all those thoughts you've had running around in your mind about what it will be like as an owner of this franchise).

You want to talk to franchise owners after you've spent a good amount time learning everything you can about the franchise so you know exactly what you want to learn more about and validate with the franchise owners. If you go into those conversations unprepared and a franchise owner senses you are unprepared, it's not going to be a productive conversation for anyone. There is an art to approaching these critical conversations. With the private candidates I work with, we spend a lot of time talking through a specific approach to these conversations that make them insanely productive. I'm talking about how to go about getting all the information you need to not only figure out the financial potential but also other well-crafted questions you can ask that gives you a ton of insight into a franchise. It's a lot more than just calling up a franchise owner and asking them how much money they've made. That approach will get you a one-way-high-speed-train-ticket to nowhere. More on this later.

**One last thing before getting
some specific funding options…**

Let's talk about <u>exit strategy</u>.

And by exit strategy, I mean what do you plan to do with the business long-term? Are you going to cash out on your hard work by selling the business or pass the business on to a family member and create a legacy?

The reason it's important to start thinking about your long-term plans for your own successful business is because when you have a successful business, you have a valuable asset that someone will pay you a premium for. This is like a 401(k) plan only better. See, as an entrepreneur, you get to triple dip:

1. The first dip is the income your business produces for you and your family;
2. The second dip is the unique retirement options you have access to that W-2 employees don't;
3. And the third dip (which is my personal favorite), is the asset you have after you've built your own successful business.

You can't sell a job but you can sell a business.

That third dip of asset creation becomes an important piece of the puzzle for you in investing in the right franchise. That's because the great franchises want their franchise owners to sell their franchises for maximum value. In fact, the truly great franchisors help their franchise owners sell their business and get maximum value. So, not only does your exit strategy become something personally to think about, it also becomes something to research by speaking with the rep you're working with and the franchise owners you speak with.

An exit strategy story.

One of the last things I did at that global franchise gig I had was help a franchise owner sell their business for almost seven-figures and capitalize on their exit strategy. This particular owner was a husband and wife team who built an education franchise over an eight-year period and sold it for a double-digit multiple of what they initially invested in the business.

Their journey started because they weren't happy with their career paths in the corporate world.

    Like many people, they started working for a company at a young age and worked their way through the corporate ladder. While they enjoyed success, they became increasingly dissatisfied with the lack of fulfillment they felt in their jobs. They wanted more flexibility during the day to attend events with their children. Frequent business trips took them away from their families which added to their frustration.

So they decided to research starting a business and they quickly realized that investing in a franchise offered them the highest opportunity for happiness, fulfillment and greater success.

    They had the desire and motivation to build their own business and were prepared to invest the hard work and sweat equity, but they didn't have the business idea. With the help of a franchise consultant, they were able to narrow down and carefully research some franchises that aligned with their goals and strengths. For a variety of personal reasons, they decided on an education franchise which was rapidly emerging at the time.

Fast forward a number of years and skip over a lot of hard work and persistence, and this husband and wife team built a business that was producing more household income than they had ever dreamed of and required less than five hours of their time per week to manage.

    The business was staffed with employees who performed every aspect of the day-to-day operation. The franchisor's marketing and lead generation processes drove a continual supply of leads for the business to convert into paying customers. This franchise (like many) also developed and provided its franchisees with a proprietary operating system that centralized and automated a lot of the administrative aspects of the business thus enabling the franchisees to operate very efficiently with less overhead and, ultimately, more cash flow.

    Operationally, this couple built and structured their franchise in a way that made the business very transferrable to a new owner. Since the business operated without their direct full-time involvement, a new owner could step into the ownership role rather seamlessly which made the business more attractive to a broader demographic of buyers (more demand = more value).

This couple will tell you that by investing in a franchise they were able to leverage the training and systems provided by the franchisor to accelerate their path to profitability and maximize their margins by using the franchise company's infrastructure and proven strategies which ultimately helped them enjoy a very healthy cash out on their exit. If it weren't for the business model, support, systems, and training provided by the franchisor, they probably wouldn't have been able to achieve what they did.

How to fund your business (the nuts and bolts stuff).

There are three major components to funding your business the right way:

1. Upfront cash out of pocket
2. Working capital
3. Personal working capital

Upfront cash out of pocket

These are expenses that you incur upfront and pay for out of the bucket of capital you have budgeted for the overall funding of the business. The franchise fee, down payments for a loan, construction costs, a budget for marketing and advertising, travel for training, vehicles, equipment or real estate lease are some examples of startup expenses in this category.

Working capital

Working capital, or "dry powder" as I like to refer to it, is the money you have set aside to cover operating expenses during the ramp-up phase until your business is producing enough cash flow to pay for itself.

Personal working capital (i.e. household expenses)

Personal working capital is the source of funds you plan to cover your personal living or household expenses with until the business is producing enough cash flow to pay for itself and then pay you.

There are a number of different options to source the funds you need to start a business.

Before I get into the specific options, I want to share something. The funding partner you work with, to help you fund your franchise, is **just as important** as the funding option you go with. I say that because you want to work with a funding partner who is **familiar** with your franchise. There are a small handful of funding companies in the U.S. that specialize in helping people fund franchises. These companies offer a variety of options (see below) and, most importantly, they know and understand the franchises they help people fund.

This last piece is important for a number of reasons and it's different for another. The reason it's different is because your local banks are typically not familiar with many franchises. This is because of a simple reason: they just don't fund many franchise deals. Work with whoever you like, but **don't** work with a funding source or bank who isn't familiar with the franchise you are trying to fund.

I have personal relationships with the top franchise funding companies in the country and my private candidates are able to take advantage of these relationships. Funding is a critical piece of the preparation component to investing in a franchise the right way so I make sure my private candidates get connected with the best funding resources to help them understand their funding options and put together the best funding strategy.

Onward to the funding options…

401(k)/IRA Funding

With 401(k)/IRA business financing (formally known as Rollovers for Business Start-ups or ROBS), you can use funds from an eligible retirement account to buy a small business or franchise without taking a taxable distribution or getting a loan.

This process is similar to buying stock in a public company, but instead, you're investing in your own privately held company. While many might believe this is a new concept, entrepreneurs have utilized this method of funding for over 30 years.

There are a handful of reputable companies in the country that specialize in helping people utilize this funding option. Contact me directly and I'll be happy to share the list.

Some of the advantages of this type of funding over other traditional methods (like loans) include:

- It's tax-deferred and penalty-free.
- You can secure funding fast – sometimes in as little as 10 business days.
- There are no interest payments or repayment of loans.
- It's debt-free or reduced-debt funding.
- You can gain cash flow and build equity faster.
- It's not dependent on your credit score.

Small Business Administration (SBA) Loans

Small Business Administration (SBA) loans offer a practical method of small business financing for entrepreneurs looking to start, buy or expand a business. You can use the funds to purchase real estate, cover construction costs or to use as working capital. SBA loans range from $500 to $5 million.

SBA small business loans offer attractive repayments terms and low interest rates. The loans are typically not directly from the SBA. Rather, the SBA encourages banks to lend to small business owners with preferable terms and multiple loan options. In return, the SBA guarantees 75% to 85% of the loan for the bank if the loan defaults.

SBA loans offer up to $5 million in financing that can be used for almost any business purpose, including start-up, acquisition or expansion. Loan proceeds can be used as working capital, revolving funds, or to purchase real estate, equipment, inventory, etc.

Additionally, SBA 7(a) loans can be combined with other forms of small business financing to help you reach your funding needs. In fact, you could even use money from your retirement account to cover the down payment for an SBA loan with 401(k) business funding.

Home equity line of credit

A home equity line of credit or HELOC can be a fast and efficient source of funds. Generally speaking, banks don't require people to supply as much documentation like business plans and projections needed for a traditional business loan.

Leasing

Leasing is typically used for equipment, furniture, computers, software, printers or other tangible items needed to operate a business. Leasing can be a good option to preserve cash and working capital.

Portfolio loans

If you own stocks, bonds, mutual funds or other eligible securities, you may be able to borrow up to 80% against the value of your portfolio without having to liquidate your holdings. Portfolio loans, also referred to as stock loans or securities-based lending, work like a revolving line of credit — allowing you to finance a business or franchise by borrowing (and repaying) at will.

Step 3:

Look In The Mirror

You know those days when you wake up and you have that feeling that you could be putting your time and energy into something of your own versus building someone else's business and dream?

Or you dread those days that are filled with meeting upon meeting upon meeting?

Or you start to hear some murmurs that "changes" are coming and you feel like a sitting duck?

Or, how about having to fight through a rough commute filled with traffic and waking up earlier and earlier and getting home later and later?

That's where the seeds of entrepreneurship start for many. But only some ever make those seeds come to fruition.

Meet Matt and Denise

Matt and Denise are private candidates of mine who I worked with last year.

Matt was a very successful corporate executive. On paper you'd think he had it made. He was rising through the ranks of a large Fortune 100 company very quickly. Making a ton of money, and by all measures an extremely successful person. He was the sole income producer and provided his family with a wonderful life.

However…he wasn't happy. He had a young family who he never saw and this was grinding him down.

He would get up at 5 AM, go workout and head into the office for a twelve-hour day, leave the office at 6 PM, sit in traffic for an hour and get home in time to have dinner and help his daughters with homework. This was the life he had to lead in order to stay on the career path he was on.

Matt's AHA Moment

One day he grabbed coffee with a former co-worker. Like Matt, his friend was on the same path as Matt – making a ton of money, rising through the ranks, but working a ton of hours and had a constant feeling of guilt and he was flat out unfulfilled. Well, a few years back this guy did a complete one-eighty in his career and invested in and opened a few locations of a massage franchise.

Everyone told him he was crazy. Why would he give up what he had to open a massage franchise? Who is going to pay a monthly membership for massages? Everyone had an opinion. He did it anyway. And it ended up being a very wise move.

See, this friend invested in a first mover, emerging franchise that ended up taking the country by storm. He was so successful with his first location he ended up opening multiple locations very quickly. He busted his butt to get good solid managers in place at each location who he empowered to run the day-to-day operations. He worked feverishly to follow the system that so many other franchise owners were having. He cranked up his marketing and advertising to drive leads into his business that converted into paying monthly customers. And he spent a lot of time establishing a very unique culture that his employees loved and became run-through-the-wall loyal.

In a few short years, this friend had created a multi-unit operation that ran on autopilot. It was a cash cow that was fueled by a lucrative recurring revenue stream and run by a solid team of managers and employees. This friend then converted this success into a very attractive lifestyle that only required him to work about 10 hours per week. And most of that was staying visible to his managers and staff and watching the numbers to make sure everything was working the way it should. This was the end goal for Matt's friend. He wanted to hustle hard for a few years to build the business to a point where it was producing more cash than he was making at his previous corporate gig and also only requiring a small amount of his time each week to run.

Well, Matt learned all about this from his friend over coffee that one day.

Matt asked his friend how he heard about this franchise and his friend told him that a franchise consultant told him about it. This franchise wasn't on anyone's radar yet, except for those people who keep an ear to the ground and look out for franchises that have the characteristics of a great franchise.

This conversation was Matt's "aha" moment.

This is where I come in…

So, Matt reached out to me. And this is where the story gets good.

At first, I wasn't ready to take Matt on as a private candidate because he had a timeline of three years. What I mean by that is Matt wanted to spend the next three years going to a job that he was beginning to seriously resent and then start his business. He was in the very early stages of research. It's not my place to tell anyone when to start a business so I gave him and his wife a few things to think about, and to get back in touch with me when they were ready to make the life change and work hard to find a great franchise.

Denise, Matt's wife was also very skeptical and very worried about this major life change. And rightfully so, it's a huge decision. So, I gently recommended they start to have some candid discussions about the reality of making such a major life change. Things like the short-term sacrifice of certain current lifestyle luxuries that a new business wouldn't be able to provide for. Stuff like that. I tried to paint as clear a picture as I could of what it would be like to build a business over a few years and get it to a point where they would have exactly what they wanted both financially and lifestyle wise.

Crossing the Mindset Chasm

Well, six months later I got a call from Matt. He told me he was ready. When I asked what he was ready for, he told me that he and Denise were ready to make the change. In my world, Matt had crossed the mindset chasm and wasn't going back (this is important and if I was a better writer, I'd call it foreshadowing).

And this where the story gets really interesting.

So I did my thing and we worked together to figure out the important characteristics for their ideal business, connected them with some funding specialists who helped them get a better idea of their options, and we got ready to dig in and do some research on some solid franchises. I came back with a few recommendations, but after a few calls with each franchisor Matt and Denise didn't find a fit. So I did another search and recommended a few more franchises. And bingo. They found one they loved.

It was a franchise with 9-5, Monday through Friday business hours. Repeat customers and recurring revenue. A relatively low investment. And what they really liked about it was the potential for it to scale. They did their research talked to a number of franchise owners and validated everything they were thinking about the business. They loved the culture and everyone on the management and support team. It was a fit. So Matt and Denise went to Discovery Day, came back, had one sleepless night thinking about if this was the right decision or not, determined it was and moved forward. They signed the franchise agreement, paid the franchise fee, and had their kick off call. Matt put a plan together to quit his job so he could get his bonus which was paid out in April and everything was set.

And then the call came. Matt's boss wanted to meet with him.

Well, this meeting was a week before Matt had planned to sit down with his boss and tell her that he was leaving the company to start his own business.

When Matt sat down with his boss he was really nervous. I mean, from what he was told he was starting to rethink everything.

And then his boss hit him with it.

She was offering him a two-band promotion. When Matt explained to me what "two-band" meant I realized how significant it was. This was the promotion he was busting his butt for and sacrificing all that time away from his family. The increase in pay alone would have more than covered the franchise fee.

So, I asked him, "What did you do?"

He told me he turned it down. And then, shared his plans with his boss.

He said his boss went white. She literally couldn't comprehend what had just happened. Can you imagine this whole thing...being offered a life changing promotion a week after you had just bought into a franchise and started your entrepreneurial journey?

When I asked Matt how he was able to make the decision so quickly, he shared how he had already checked out mentally of the corporate world and was in the entrepreneurial mindset (in other words, he had crossed the mindset chasm). He was done with the corporate life. He also explained how the promotion would have meant more work, more travel, and ultimately, more time away from his family. The money just wasn't worth it.

Fast forward to today and Matt is putting more energy into his business than he ever put into his former job. He is home to put his daughters off to school, is home for dinner, can step away to attend whatever school events his daughters have, has a fifteen-minute commute and is **happy**. He and Denise have their business on a great trajectory and are the happiest they've been in a long time.

You may be wondering why I just shared Matt and Denise's story with you.

The reason is their story ties into another important step to approaching business ownership in prepared way. And what it specifically has to do with is figuring out your **WHY**.

Business ownership is an opportunity for many people to create something for themselves and achieve the vision they have for themselves and their family. Everyone's vision (or **WHY**) is different and highly personal. Some people want to spend more time with their families and get off the road. Some people want to stop building wealth for other people and shareholders, and build an asset for themselves. Some people want to put their skills and abilities to use in their own business and get away from the trials and tribulations of working in large corporations.

Whatever it is you want to achieve, the first step is identifying it and rolling it into a vision. Your vision will become your passion that fuels you to achieve it.

By starting with your **WHY** and creating a vision that you can get passionate about you're setting yourself up for success in whatever business you decide to start. These two key elements will help open your mind to business opportunities that you may have overlooked and ultimately lead you down the right path to determining which business is going to get you where you want to be.

Step #4:

Buying The Right Franchise

Now on to the fun part...

Finding some great franchises to research.

In this section, you're going to learn about the different options you have to find franchises. They each have their pros and cons which I'll talk to you about. Before your search for a franchise, it's important to know what you're looking for in a franchise.

In the world of franchising you have a lot of options. Not all of them are great so I'll give you a crash course on the landscape.

First things first, in order for a company to offer a franchise of their business they have to have two things both of which are required by the Federal Trade Commission. They are:

1. Trademark their brand
2. Issue a Franchise Disclosure Document

Now, it's also important to understand that while the FTC governs franchising, and a company must have these two things and abide by the FTC guidelines and laws, there is no approval process. Meaning as long as a company is complying with the FTC guidelines, issuing an FDD to prospective franchise owners and has acquired their trademark, a company can franchise. In other words, there are no quality standards. So franchising essentially offers a mini-free market where the strong survive and thrive and the others do their thing. This is why it's very important for you to know what to look for so you can spot the great franchises.

In the U.S., there are over 3,000 different franchise brands available.

Think about that for a second. Three thousand!

About half are food, hotels and real estate franchises and the other half span 80 different industries ranging from disaster restoration franchises to education franchises to fitness to beauty to automotive and everything in between. This latter 1,500 or so franchise concepts (i.e. what I refer to as the non-food side), generally don't require any direct industry experience. The great franchises in this category certainly do not!

Now, of the 1,500 or so franchises in the "non-food" side, you're going to have your top performers (i.e. what I refer to as "great franchises"), your average performers, and your bottom performers. Obviously, you want to focus on the top performers.

A <u>great</u> franchise should have:

- A rock-solid business model with phenomenal margins and economics
- Outstanding support for their owners
- A talented and dedicated leadership team
- Cutting-edge tools that their franchise owners use to run their businesses more efficiently (which allows more money to hit the bottom line)
- An amazing culture, and, most importantly,
- A bunch (and by a *bunch* I mean **<u>a lot</u>**) of very happy and very profitable franchise owners.

Now, you know what's interesting? None of the criteria I just mentioned is actually measured in a reliable way by any of these "franchise ranking" experts. Entrepreneur Magazine's Franchise 500, which is the most famous ranking, evaluates franchises by what's in their FDD. Which is silly because the FDD doesn't disclose anything about culture, the business model, the happiness or profitability of their franchises, etc. It's a black and white document with a bunch of template information that attorneys charge franchisors an arm and leg for that typically doesn't reflect the operational reality of what it's really like to own that franchise and be a part of the company.

You can probably tell I have a strong opinion about the franchise rankings. I just think it adds a lot of noise out there. Then again, it's kind of why my job exists so maybe I should be happy it's there.

Regardless. Onward.

Before you start your search, do this.

So, now that you have a quick introduction to the nuts and bolts of franchising and I've shared my criteria for **great** franchises, let's talk about figuring out what you're looking for first before I talk about where to go find it.

What I'm referring to is figuring out the key criteria for you and your ideal franchise business.

This is one of the areas that I spend a lot of time working with my private candidates on. It's kind of like the first time you bought your first house (or any house for that matter). There were probably certain things like four bedrooms, two-and-a-half bath minimum, quality construction, updated kitchen and bathrooms, big yard, quiet street, great schools, within the budget and so on. Searching for a great franchise is similar, just with a different set of criteria.

But it's critical to talk through the different options because most of this stuff isn't talked about much. That's why I spend a lot of time working through these details upfront because it sets the stage for focusing on the right franchises.

The important criteria:

Budget – how much are you comfortable investing?

Speed to positive cash flow – How fast do you need or want to start making money out of the business? Low overhead franchises are faster and brick-and-mortar franchises take more time (but the latter open the option to keep your job while you build the business…see "semi-absentee" below).

Single or multi-units – Basically, that's a fancy way of saying do you want one location or multiple? Most mobile service-based franchises or home-based franchises are single unit opportunities with the ability to purchase additional territory if you want to expand. Brick and mortar franchises can offer multi-unit opportunities where you agree to open multiple locations of that franchise, just like Matt's friend did with the massage franchise. Interestingly, many multi-unit franchise owners find it easier to run multiple locations versus just one location.

Customer acquisition – An important one. Do you want a business that thrives off inbound marketing that drives leads to your franchise or would you rather be the face-of-the-franchise in your community?

Full-time or semi-absentee ownership - In other words, how much time do you want to invest? There are great franchises that require the owner to work in the business full-time in order to get it to a point where they might be able to take a step back. Conversely, there are semi-absentee (which is a franchise industry word for manager-run) franchises that require a "part-time" time commitment from the owners because the franchise is run by a manager. Semi-absentee franchises enable owners to keep their job (i.e. W-2 income).

The type of business – Investing in a particular franchise is a very personal decision. You're going to have certain preferences whether you realize it or not. The only way to really figure out the types of franchises you'd be open to is to start researching some. I'm a big believer that the most fail-safe and scientific method to investing in the right franchise for you is to research 3-4 high-quality franchises, compare them to one another, contrast them against one another and you'll start to figure out what you really like and don't like. There is no shortcut for that, I promise.

This is just a sampling of some important criteria. My private candidates and I spend a lot of time talking through these and more, but you should have an idea of what I'm trying to get you to think about.

Where do you find the great franchises?

The easiest and most reliable way to find great franchises to research is to become a private candidate of mine (I'll tell you more about how you can do that at the end of this book). You have some other options as well.

Google – When you start Googling you'll find a lot of different franchisors that do direct advertising. You'll also find a bunch of different "franchise directories" which are basically lead generators that sell leads to those franchisors who advertise on them.

Franchise rankings – By now you probably have an idea of my opinion of franchise rankings. We disagree on what makes a franchise a truly top franchise. The franchise ranking websites are all franchise directories as well where franchisors can pay to advertise. It's pretty much a pay-for-play system. I used to spend a lot of money advertising on these franchise directories so I know the belly of the beast. I'm not saying they are all bad, they just aren't as pure as they position themselves. None of them rank franchise on the fundamentals that truly makes them great. If you submit your information on one of these sites, one of two things will happen.

1. You're going to get called and emailed quickly. Sometimes by the franchise you requested information about and sometimes by other franchisors (some directories will sell your "lead" to a few different franchises). Be ready.

Or,

2. You won't hear anything.

The best way to get information about a particular franchise is to go to the franchise section on their website.

Trade shows – These are becoming less and less prevalent each year. I'm not a fan of them because it's typically a cattle show where there are a bunch of franchise sales reps manning their ten-by-ten booth awkwardly trying to talk to people perusing the aisles. They are uncomfortable. You may get lucky, but I'd rather put my money on a lottery ticket.

Franchise consultants (like yours truly) – you get the point by now.

The Research Process

After you've found a few high-quality franchises, it's time to dig in and dissect them. To get every detail you want, you're going to walk through a few steps which I'll touch on. But, before I get into that, know that the great franchises are evaluating you as well. It's a process of mutual evaluation. It's kind of like dating and figuring out if you want to get married. The goal is to figure out if there is a good two-way-long-term fit.

In reality, you're going to be sold a bit by the sales rep you'll be working with. That's ok. Just expect it. You're still going to be able to get all of the details you need to figure it out if you follow these steps.

I'm going to give a quick overview of the steps. There is a lot more that goes into each one of these steps in order to get the information you want. I obviously spend a lot of time with my private candidates reviewing this approach and coaching them on how to approach each step. Generally speaking, you're looking at a couple of hours each week that needs to be dedicated to researching franchises over a 4-6 week period.

The steps in my research process are:

1. **Open a dialogue with the franchisor** – this is where you'll start working with a sales rep. The goal here is to learn as much as you can about the franchise from the top down.

2. **Franchise Disclosure Document Review** – once you've had a conversation or two with the sales rep, they are going to send you the FDD. You'll want to review it, especially Items 3,4,6,7 and 19.

3. **Talk to franchise owners** – this is where you're going to spend most of your time and rightfully so. There is somewhat of an art to having these conversations. You're going to want to have as many conversations with franchise owners you need to in order to feel comfortable. If you're hearing a lot of inconsistencies or don't identify with these owners, it's best to walk away and find another franchise to research.

4. **Attend a Discovery Day** – these are called Discovery Days, Meet the Team Days, Join the Team Days, and a bunch of other names but the point is this is the step in the process where you go to the franchise's headquarters and meet the leadership and the folks you'll be working with. It's a chance for everyone to meet in person. It's also the last step. If you follow steps one

thru three, you'll be very prepared to make a decision after attending this meeting.

5. **Make a decision** – This is where it gets emotional and scary and that's ok - it's natural. We all experience it. Just be prepared for the feelings of uncertainty and rely on your WHY and research to make the best decision for you and your family.

That's it.
That's all you have to do.
It's that simple.

Believe it or not, the actual nuts and bolts of how to do the research are the **easiest** part!

The attitude through which you approach starting your own business and investing in a franchise is the **most important** part.

And the **hardest** part is making that final decision to move forward, take a bit of a leap, and trust in the research you've done.

If you've approached this decision in the right way, with the right reason, from the beginning, the decision happens a heck of a lot more naturally than otherwise. Candidly, this is why I spent 75% of this book talking about the steps you need to take to prepare you for this journey. It matters.

If you're **serious** about owning your own successful business, here's what to do next...

(Flip the page)

Are you ready to take the next step?

(hint: it's a pretty simple one)

Now look friend, if you're truly serious about figuring out if there is a franchise out there that can help you get everything you want in life, you should get in touch with me.

You see, I've spent the last 13 years helping people invest in, build, grow and sell (as in cash out) high-quality franchises. I rub shoulders with the founders and CEOs of these high-quality franchises all the time. I know about the next high-quality emerging franchise before the media does. Yada, yadda.

My point is, I'm connected in franchising and have been doing this a long time. And that's what the people who work with me want. They want my knowledge, experience and time to, ultimately, help them save time and focus on the high-quality franchises so they can find the right one. And you know, what? **I'm happy to give it to them** (and you).

So, back to you. If you have the **mindset** and you're prepared to **invest the money** (in the right franchise) and you have a crystal-clear idea of **WHY** you want to own your own business and you're committed to putting the work in to find the **right franchise to buy**, then we should talk, because I can help you.

Become a private candidate

The first step to becoming a private candidate is a pretty simple one: We have a conversation. After we speak, we'll know if there is a good fit to work together. Again, my service is 100% free to you and you never sign a contract.

Here's what to do if you want to take the first step and have a conversation...

(flip the page one last time)

If you want to talk to me about franchising…

You can go to my website and get in touch with me that way. My website is www.DruCarpenito.com

Or, you can email me at Dru@DruCarpenito.com. Please tell me a little bit about yourself and what has you thinking about starting your own business.

From there, I'll be in touch to schedule a call to talk further.

And there you have it!

Thanks for reading my book. Now, get to work!

Cheers,

www.ingramcontent.com/pod-product-compliance
Lightning Source LLC
Chambersburg PA
CBHW070841220526
45466CB00002B/847